You-Can-Do
Bible Activity Sheets

You-Can-Do Bible Activity Sheets

Reproducible cut-and-paste activities and puzzle
forms for children's church, Sunday schools,
DVBS, and Bible Clubs

Mary Currier

BAKER BOOK HOUSE
Grand Rapids, Michigan 49516

Copyright © 1990 by Baker Books
a division of Baker Book House Company
P.O. Box 6287, Grand Rapids, MI 49516-6287

ISBN: 0-8010-2552-4

Seventh printing, May 1996

Printed in the United States of America

Special Days

1. Advent Calendar

Here are stars for every day in December until Christmas. Starting with number 1 on December 1, color a star yellow (or use a gummed star) each day.

2. Advent Poster

On December 1, glue a cotton ball on the number 1 on the lamb. Each day, glue on another cotton ball on that date until Christmas Day, December 25.

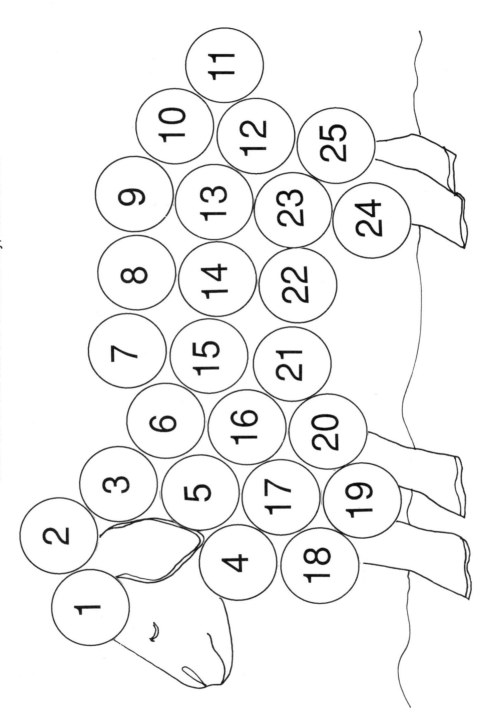

This is the time of the year we remember Jesus' birth. Jesus is also called the Lamb of God. He died to take away our sins so we can go to heaven and be with him.

3. Missing Objects

There are ten things left out of the second picture. Can you find them?

4. Star Maze

Help the wise men get through the maze to the young child, Jesus.

5. How to Draw Stars

How to make a star.

In the picture below, fill the sky with stars. Then color the picture.

6. How to Draw Sheep

The night Jesus was born, there were shepherds taking care of their sheep in the fields near Bethlehem.

You can draw a sheep by following the instructions below.

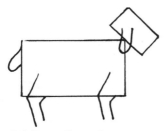

Pressing lightly with your pencil, draw a rectangle.

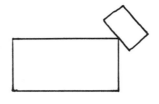

Add another as shown.

Make legs.

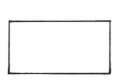

Add a tail and an ear.

Add wool as shown.

Add facial features and hooves; then erase unnecessary lines.

Draw your sheep here.

9. The Angel's Message

Circle all the words of Luke 2:10 in this puzzle.

```
       O Y P U
      E E F E A R
      B U T O L D
      R O I P Y M
    S A I D R L O A I S
    T P N J B E U N T O
    A T G O O D S W E N
    T H E Y K S I A E M
    H A D I N G S N L L
    T E T R F O R R G L U S
    V M H A L L E U E I K T
    A D I A R F A F L W E U
    N O G O N O T C I E H T
```

"But the angel said to them, 'Do not be afraid. I bring you good news of great joy that will be for all the people.'"

10. Luke 19:10

Put the words in the right order to form Luke 19:10.

_____ _____ _____ _____ _____ _____ _____ _____ _____

_____ _____ _____ _____ _____ _____ _____ _____.

11. Christmas Basket

Color the basket and handle and cut out on solid lines. Fold handle lengthwise on the dotted line, with holly leaves on the outside, and glue together. Form the basket into a cone and paste or tape. Attach the handle. Fill with small candy or other goodies and hang on the Christmas tree.

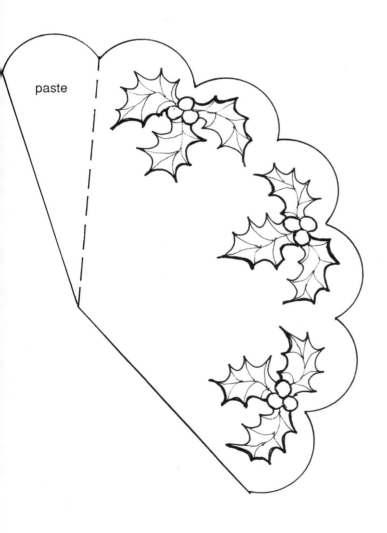

paste

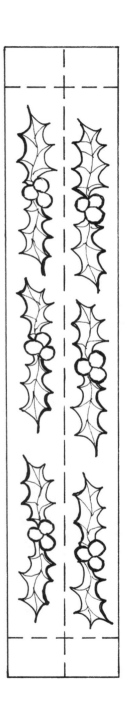

12. Christmas Lights

THE LIGHT
OF THE
WORLD
IS
JESUS

13. The Angel's Message

Connect the dots to see what the angel told the shepherds; then color the picture.

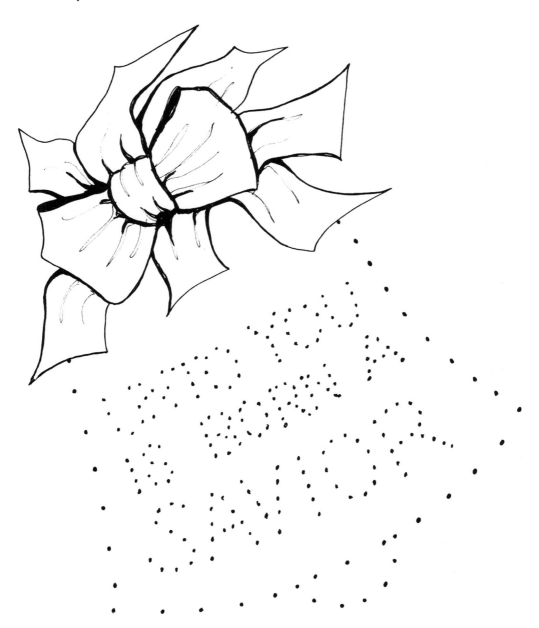

14. Straw Maze

Find your way through the straw maze. What is the baby's name?

____ ____ ____ ____ ____ ____

15. Hidden Pictures

Find 3 stars, 2 bells, 1 angel, 3 crosses, 1 staff, and 2 candles hidden in the manger.

16. The Gift of God's Love

Find the answer to the following question by using the code in the letters on the present.

God's love was shown to us by sending

——— ——— ——— ——— ———
  D   O   V   E   S

17. The Reason for Christmas

Trace over the letters and color the picture.

18. Christmas Promise

For to us a
child
is born,
to us a
Son
is given

Isaiah 9:6

Trace the letters and color the picture.

19. Christmas Doubles

Circle two pictures in each row that are the same.

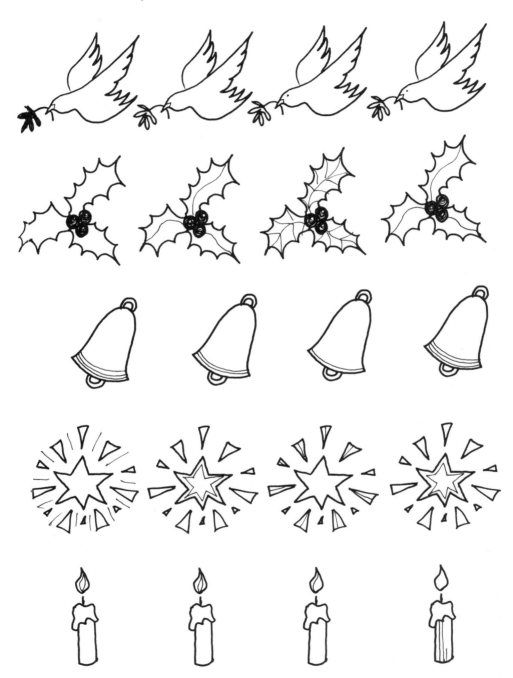

20. Angels' Message

Unscramble the words to find out what the angels said at Christ's birth.

RYGLO OT DGO NI HET GEHHITS!

"

— — — — — — — —

— — — — — — — — — —

"

— — — — — — — — —

21. Christmas Wreath

Color the picture using the following code.

B
Jesus wants me to tell others about him.

A
Jesus wants me to obey him.

Jesus died for my sin.
C

Jesus is the center of Christmas

Jesus loves me.
E

Jesus wants me to be honest.
D

Jesus wants me to love him.
F

G
Jesus wants me to live for him.

A

A—red   C—yellow   E—blue   G—purple
B—white   D—green   F—orange

22. Sign Maze

"This will be a sign to you: You will find a baby wrapped in cloths and lying in a manger."
Luke 2:12

Signs tell us what to do and where to go. The angel gave the shepherds a sign that would show they had found the baby Jesus.

Help the shepherd through the sign maze.

23. Jesus' Age When He Died

Add the numbers in the picture to find out how old Jesus was when he died on the cross. Then color the picture.

Do your figuring here.

24. Crown of Thorns Maze

Use a crayon or pencil to find your way through the crown of thorns.

"The soldiers twisted together a crown of thorns, and put it on his head."
John 19:2

25. For Whom Did Jesus Die?

Jesus died for many kinds of people. Circle those you can find in the picture (there are 24); then write them down on the lines below.

_____   _____   _____
_____   _____   _____
_____   _____   _____
_____   _____   _____
_____   _____   _____
_____   _____   _____
_____   _____   _____

26. Paper Plate Crosses

Materials:

two 9" paper plates   crayons
scissors   glue or stapler
pencil

Cut out the cross pattern on the next page. Trace onto one of the paper plates and cut out. On the back side of the plate, color the crosses brown and the hill green, or color it all black for a shadow effect.

Next, color the other plate on the front side according to the following instructions:

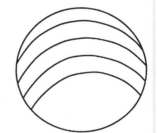

1. The coloring should look like an evening sky. Starting about one-third of the way up from the bottom of the plate, color up about an inch using a red crayon. Color in a semicircular motion, gradually lightening up.
2. Using an orange crayon, continue coloring, first going over a little into the red area. Press firmly at first and then lighten up as you continue to color in a semicircular motion about an inch.
3. Using a yellow crayon, repeat step 2, ending by coloring very lightly.
4. Finish coloring the plate with your blue crayon, using a light blue and then gradually pressing heavily around the top rim of the plate.

Glue or staple the rims of the plates together, the three crosses in front of the sky scene.

Fold an 8 1/2 x 11
sheet of paper in half.
Place the dotted edge
of the pattern on the
folded edge of the
paper. Staple the top,
bottom, and outside
edges. Cut along the
solid lines, unfold the
paper to reveal the full
pattern.

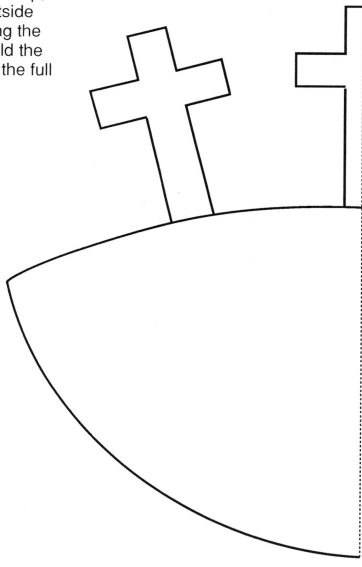

27. Christ Is Risen

28. Easter Look-Alikes

Circle the two look-alikes in each row.

29. Easter Window

Color each shape with a number in it according to the key below.

1-green
2-brown

3-red
4-blue

5-purple
6-yellow

30. Mark 6:1–8

Hidden in the puzzle below are words from Mark 16:1–8, where we read the story of Jesus rising from the grave. Try to find all the words listed at the bottom of the page.

```
            L O F T O T R
        C B A S Z O S P I C E S
        T N I O N A T A G F C C
      P Q A Z D R A H X D H E S D
      K S U N R I S E F G T B S U
S B E A B P T U W L E K R O L L E D
T F E S A B B A T H R S T R S C V W
O B W A T Q D E L F A B M O T F N L
N T K S C M A R Y H
E C R U C I F I E D
M H I R Q P I O O A
J E S U S S R S T Y
Z V E T I U S V O P
W Q N U A C T R X S
```

SABBATH	TOMB	CRUCIFIED
SPICES	STONE	RISEN
ANOINT	ROLLED	LAID
FIRST	RIGHT	FLED
DAY	ROBE	WEEK
SUNRISE	JESUS	MARY

31. Angel at the Tomb

To find out what the angel said to the women at the tomb, unscramble the words in the opening.

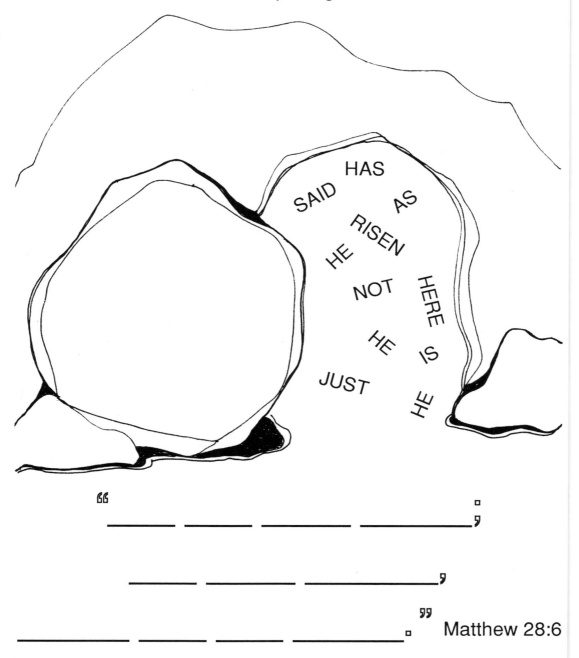

HAS
SAID
AS
HE RISEN
NOT HERE
HE IS
JUST HE

" _____ _____ _____ _____,"

_____ _____ _____;

_____ _____ _____ _____." Matthew 28:6

32. Easter Joy

Trace over the dotted lines and color the picture.

33. Jesus Said . . .

What did Jesus say before he returned to heaven? The answer is in the cloud below. Starting with the first letter, write every other letter on the lines below.

```
G S O T I B N R T Y O M A P L W L C T Z H N E L W
Q O V R G L S D T A V N A D W P Q R M E U A D C X
H I T K H J E W G S O P O R D V N T E J W M S A T
R O C A J L Q L Z C H R X E P A W T S I N O R N
```

66

—— —— ——— ——— —— —— —— — —

—— —— ——— ——— —— ——— ———————

—— ———— ——— ——— ——— —— —— ——

—— ——— ——— ———— ——— ——— —— — 99

—— —— ———— ——— ——— ——— —— ——— ——.

Mark 16:15

34. What Happened at Pentecost?

Count the number of dots in each space. Then use the letters to decode the message below about what happened at Pentecost. Check your work with Acts 2:4.

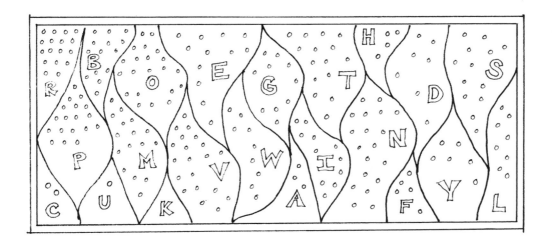

"

$\overline{3\ \ 8\ \ 8}$ $\overline{21\ \ 5}$ $\overline{15\ \ 4\ \ 12\ 16}$ $\overline{9\ \ 12\ 17\ 12}$ $\overline{5\ \ 11\ \ 8\ \ 8\ \ 12\ 7}$

$\overline{9\ \ 11\ 15\ \ 4}$ $\overline{15\ \ 4\ \ 12}$ $\overline{4\ \ 21\ \ 8\ \ 6}$ $\overline{13\ 18\ 11\ 17\ 11\ 15}$ $\overline{3\ \ 19\ \ 7}$

$\overline{14\ 12\ 10\ \ 3\ \ 19}$ $\overline{15\ 21}$ $\overline{13\ 18\ 12\ \ 3\ \ 0}$ $\overline{11\ 19}$ $\overline{21\ 15\ \ 4\ \ 12\ 17}$

$\overline{15\ 21\ 19\ 10\ \ 1\ \ 12\ 13}$ $\overline{3\ \ 13}$ $\overline{15\ \ 4\ \ 12}$ $\overline{13\ 18\ 11\ 17\ 11\ 15}$

$\overline{12\ 19\ \ 3\ \ 14\ \ 8\ \ 12\ 7}$ $\overline{15\ \ 4\ \ 12\ 16}$."

35. Jesus' Promise

Jesus made a promise before he went back to heaven. To find out what it was, fill in the blanks with the first letter of the picture below the line.

Jesus promised he will

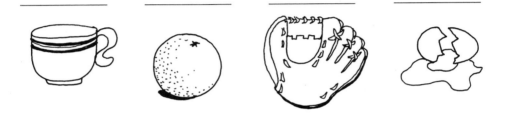

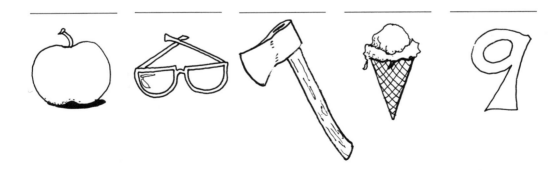

36. Jesus Is Coming Again

Connect the dots and then color the picture.

37. Christ's Return

Before Jesus went back to heaven, he told us to watch for his return. Matthew 24:36–46 tells about Christ's return. Some words from that passage are found in the puzzle below. Circle the words as you find them.

```
        A S F A
      S E R V A N T B
      O M E H I D H L
    A N A A O T W I H K
    U I N D U H I E A N
    P R A Y R F S F O O
    W A T C H U E O N W
    R O N Z L O R D
    K C O M I N G O
        E D A Y
```

COMING	THIEF	UP	PRAY
DAY	WATCH	DO	KNOW
SERVANT	ARK	LORD	FOR
MAN	HOUR	WISE	ON
IN	FAITHFUL	READY	
NOAH	SON	AN	

44

38. A Promise

What did Jesus promise when he went back to heaven? To find the answer, write the first letter of the picture on the line above it.

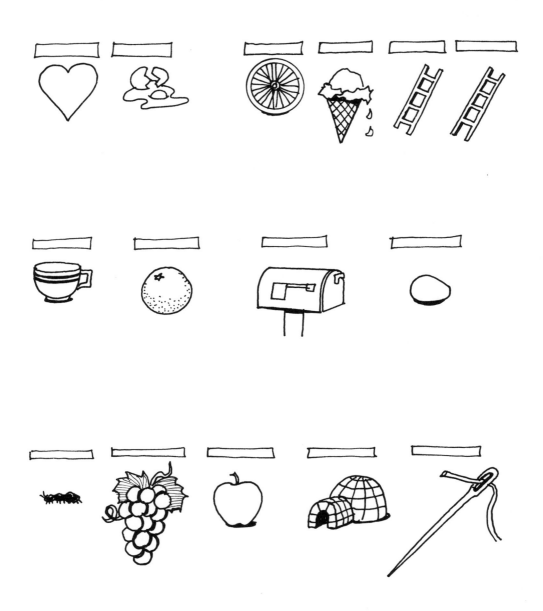

39. Valentine Shadow Box

Materials needed: crayons, glue, scissors

Color A and B. Cut out on solid lines. Fold on broken lines. Apply glue on the underside of the tabs and attach to the back of the Bible verse (A).

A

example of finished shadow box

B

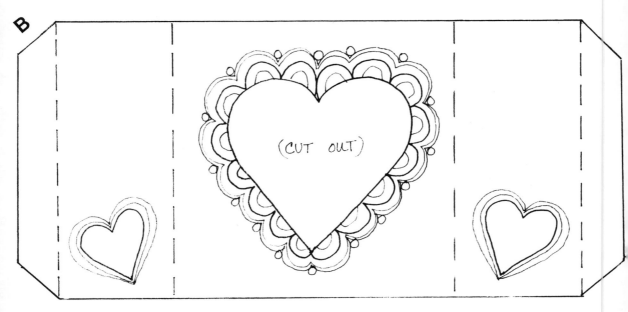

(CUT OUT)

40. Love the Lord

Trace the words, then color the picture.

41. Count the Hearts

How many hearts can you find in the picture below?

I found_____ hearts.
Color the picture.

42. Heart Wreath

Use the code at the bottom of the page to fill in the blanks in the heart wreath. Then on each heart write a way that you can be friendly to others.

— · LOVES   — · — FRIEND
·· — ALL   — — · TIMES
· — A   ·· AT

43. Mother's Day Picture to Color

44. A Good Rule

Using the code, write the words of 1 Thessalonians 5:18 on the lines in the frame.

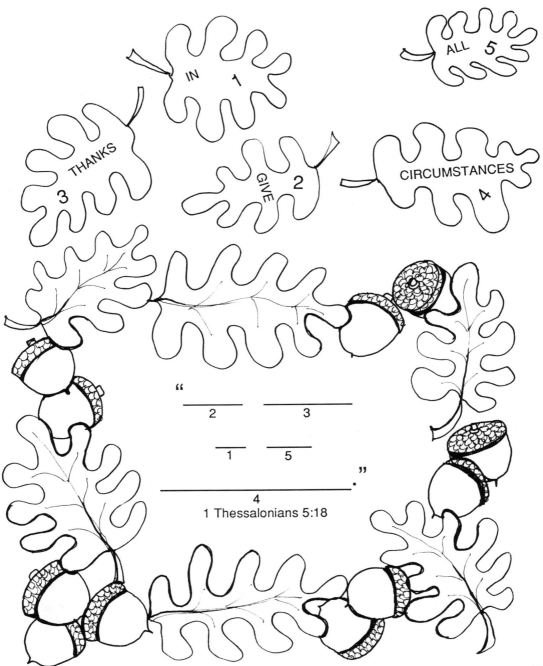

IN 1

ALL 5

THANKS 3

GIVE 2

CIRCUMSTANCES 4

"___ ___
2   3

___ ___
1   5

_____."
4
1 Thessalonians 5:18

51

45. Psalm 107:1

On the line below each leaf write the word that appears in the matching leaf at the top of the page.

Key

46. Dinner Word Scramble

Often we celebrate Thanksgiving Day with friends and relatives by having a big dinner. Unscramble the words in the dishes and write them on the lines below.

_____   _____

_____   _____

_____   _____

_____   _____

_____   _____

47. Thanksgiving Word Scramble

We have many things to be thankful for. Unscramble the letters in the apples to find out what some of them are. Write the words on the lines below the basket.

_____   _____   _____

_____   _____   _____

_____   _____   _____

48. Origami Dove

"As soon as Jesus was baptized, he went up out of the water. At that moment heaven was opened, and he saw the Spirit of God descending like a dove and lighting on him. And a voice from heaven said, 'This is my Son, whom I love; with him I am well pleased.'"   Matthew 3:16–17

Follow the instructions below to make a dove out of paper.

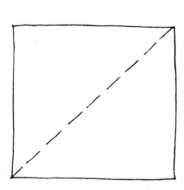

1. Fold a square paper diagonally.

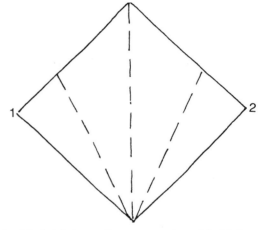

2. Unfold, turn the paper, and fold 1 and 2 toward the center fold.

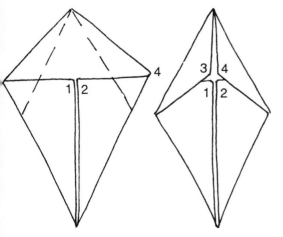

3. Fold 3 and 4 as shown.

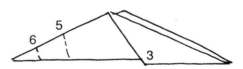

4. Fold the project in half along the first fold line so that 3 and 4 are on the outside. Then fold at 5 and 6.

5. Push in toward the center as shown to form the neck and head. With a pen draw on two eyes.

55

49. Jesus' Baptism

After Jesus was baptized, God sent the Holy Spirit in the shape of a _____. (Read Matt. 3:16.)

Draw exactly what you see in each box into the same numbered square at the bottom of the page.

50. Jesus' Life

Draw a line from the words at the left to the matching picture at the right.

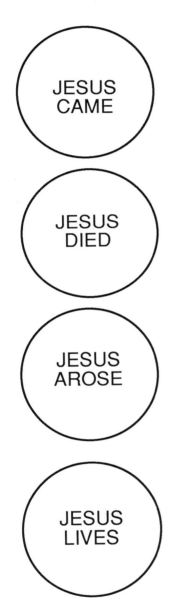

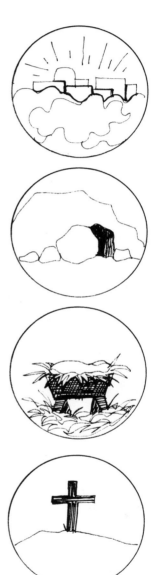

51. Jesus' Baptism

To find the form the Holy Spirit took at Jesus' baptism, connect the dots. Then color the picture.

52. Salvation Message

To find the answer to the question in the center of this puzzle, start with the letter "B" in the center of the picture and write down every other letter on the lines below.

— — — — — — — — — —   — — —   — — — —

— — — — —   — — — — — —

53. Luke 10:2

Jesus wants us to tell other people about how to be saved. Read Luke 10:2 and fill in the blanks.

"He [Jesus] told them, 'The _____ is _____,

but the _____ are few. _____ the

_____ of the _____, therefore, to send

out _____ into his _____

field.'"

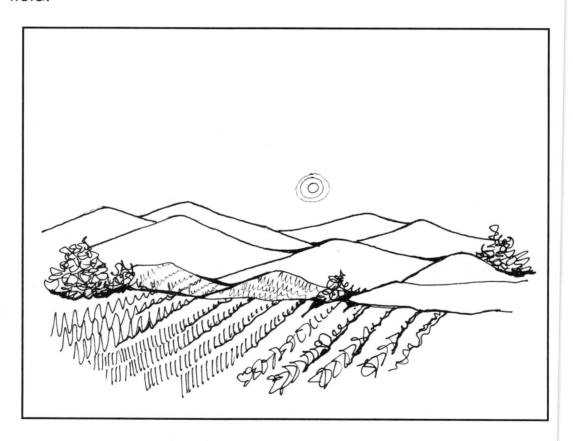

54. Coded Message

Use the code below to find out what Acts 15:11 tells us about salvation.

"

_____   _____   _____
8   2   12

_____   _____   _____
10   1   14

_____   _____   _____
5   11   3

_____   _____
9   4

_____   _____   _____
6   8   13

"
_____ .
7

THROUGH	GRACE	OUR	SAVED	IT	WE	OF	LORD	THAT	THE	BELIEVE	IS	JESUS	ARE
1	5	3	7	12	8	11	9	6	14	2	10	4	13

55. Color by Number

Color the picture using the code below.

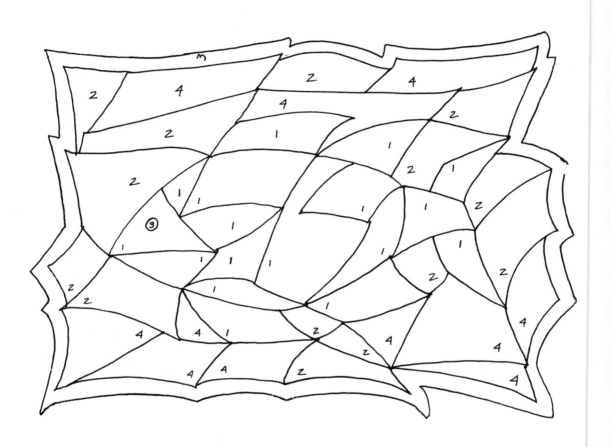

1 - yellow   3 - black
2 - blue   4 - green

Jesus said we should follow him, and he will make us fishers of men.

56. The Way to Heaven

There is only one way to get to heaven. It is by believing and trusting in

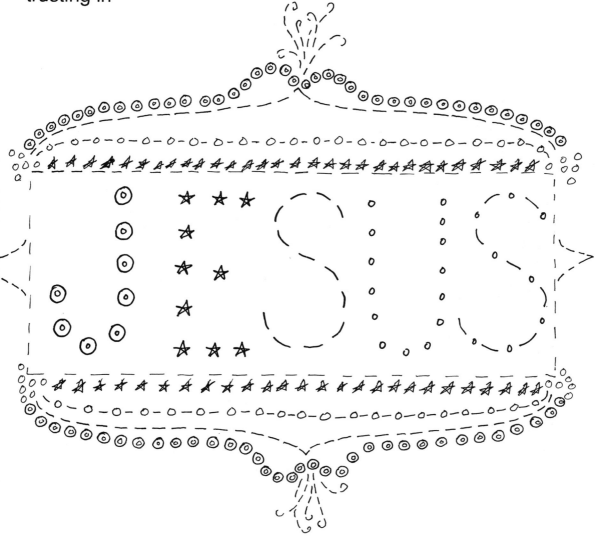

Trace over the ⓞ with a blue crayon.
Trace over the ⚔ with a green crayon.
Trace over the --- with a yellow crayon.
Trace over the ₒ with an orange crayon.
Trace over the ₒ-ₒ- with a red crayon.

63

57. How to Be Saved

"Believe in the Lord Jesus, and you will be saved."
Acts 16:31

58. The Best Gift

What is the best gift of all? Do the puzzle below to find out.

The last letter in _____

The first letter in _____

The third letter in _____

The first letter in _____

The second letter in _____

The first letter in _____

The second letter in _____

The second letter in _____

The third letter in _____

59. Psalm 10:16

Circle the phrase "The Lord Is King" and color the crown.

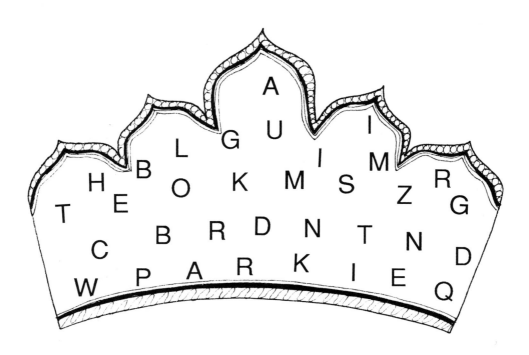

Trace over the letters of this Bible verse.

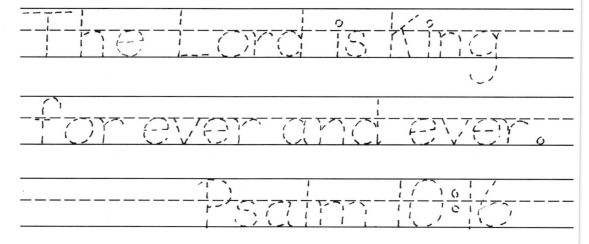

The Lord is King

for ever and ever.

Psalm 10:16

60. Proverbs 20:11

"EVEN A CHILD IS KNOWN BY HIS ACTIONS."

PROVERBS 20:11

61. Isaiah 55:6

"SEEK THE LORD WHILE HE MAY BE FOUND."

ISAIAH 55:6

62. Life Through Jesus

We have new life through the death and resurrection of Jesus.
Circle all of the things that grow.

63. Luke 21:33

Match the numbers under the lines with the numbers in the globe.
Write the words from the globe on the lines.

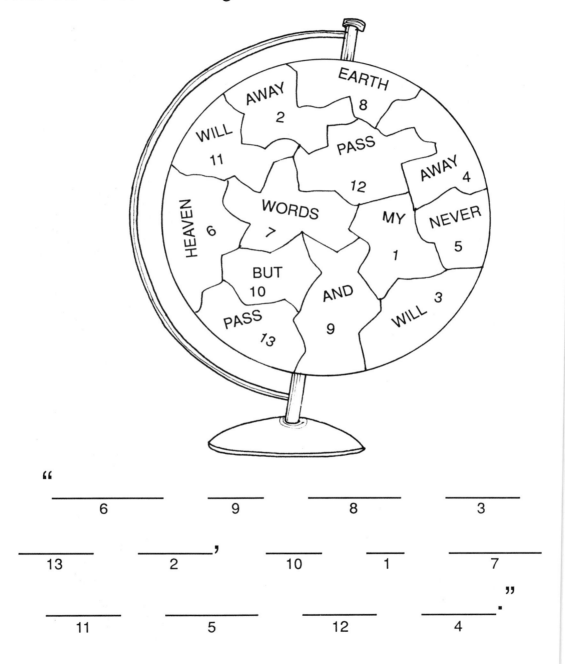

"

_____ _____ _____ _____
    6   9   8   3

_____ _____' _____ _____ _____
  13   2   10   1   7

"
_____ _____ _____ _____.
  11   5   12   4

64. Treasures in Heaven

To draw a squirrel in the tree below, follow the instructions.

Pressing lightly with your pencil, start with an oval as shown.

Add a smaller oval.

Add legs as shown.

Erase unnecessary lines and add eyes and mouth.

Make a tail and ears.

Add small details as shown.

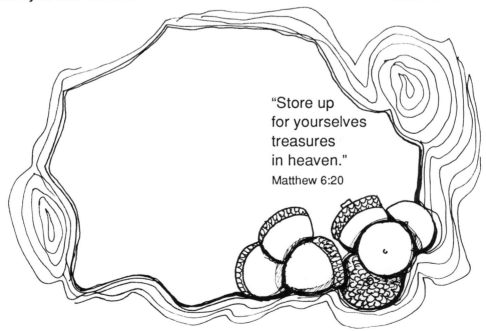

"Store up for yourselves treasures in heaven."

Matthew 6:20

65. Who Forgives Sin?

Do the puzzle below to find out who forgives your sins.

Look at each picture. Subtract the letters and write the letter that is left.

JAR − AR = ___

KITE − KIT = ___

FISH − FIH = ___

SUN − SN = ___

STAR − TAR = ___

66. Philippians 4:19

"MY GOD WILL MEET ALL YOUR NEEDS."

67. Luke 4:8

Find the following objects hidden in the picture below: egg, ball, baseball bat, cup, star, fish, kite, umbrella, pencil, orange, spoon, and ice cream cone.

68. Missing Letters

Find the missing letter in each word, then write the words correctly on the lines at the bottom of the page.

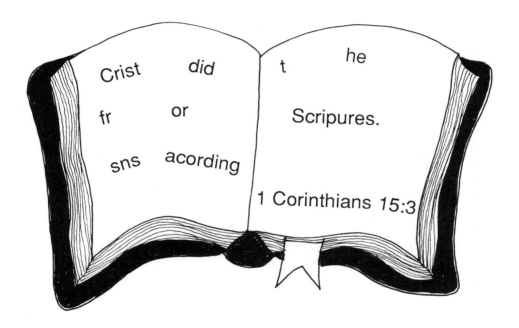

Crist   did   t   he

fr   or   Scripures.

sns   acording

1 Corinthians 15:3

_____

_____

69. Peter

Peter loved Jesus and wanted to do right, but sometimes he found himself in situations where his emotions took over.

Draw what Peter may have looked like in the passage under each blank face. Use the examples below.

Mark 14:29   Mark 14:37   Mark 14:66–68

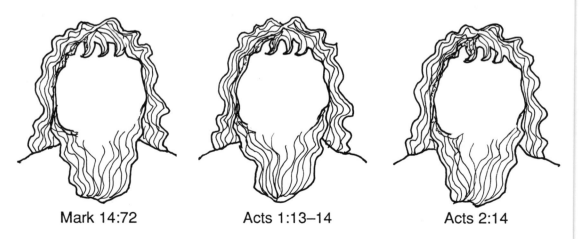

Mark 14:72   Acts 1:13–14   Acts 2:14

70. The Lord's Supper

At the Lord's Supper, Jesus told the disciples that he would soon die on the cross for the sins of the world. He said we should remember his death. When we celebrate the Lord's Supper, we drink the grape juice as a memorial of Jesus dying on the cross.

Color the two cup patterns below gold or silver on both sides and cut out. Put together as shown to stand up.

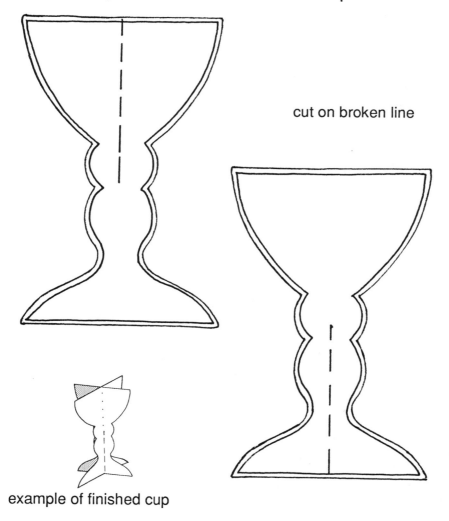

cut on broken line

example of finished cup

"This cup is the new covenant in my blood, which is poured out for you." Luke 22:20

77

71. Hidden Letters

Jesus promised to send someone to help us when he went back to heaven. Find all the letters in the picture above. Then unscramble them to get your answer.

___ ___ ___ ___   ___ ___ ___ ___ ___ ___

72. Luke 2:10

Fill in the blanks at the bottom of this page using the code found in the large word **JOY**.

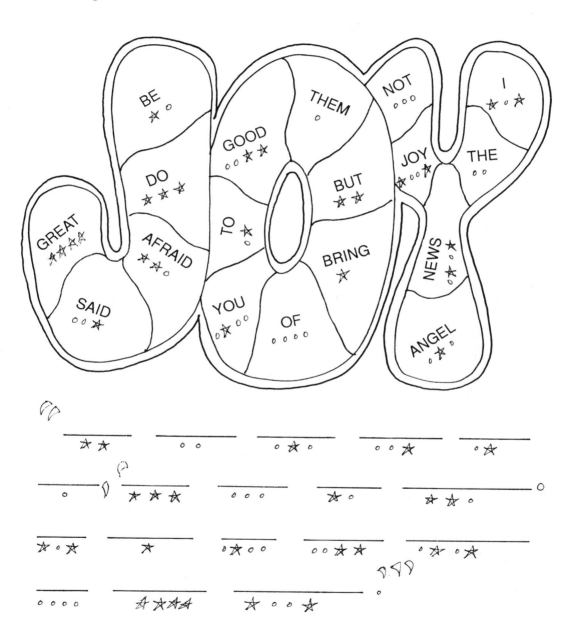

73. Freedom to Worship

Where do we have freedom to worship God? Unscramble the letters in the window to find the answer.

—— —— —— —— —— ——

74. Origami House

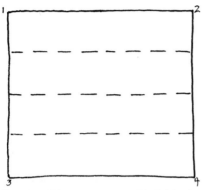

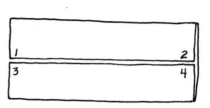

Fold ends toward the
center as shown.

Start with a square. Fold in half
and then in half again. Unfold.

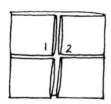

Fold backward toward the
center and turn around.

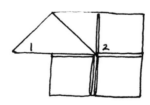

Pull out points 1 and 2
and crease.

Stand up.

75. Origami Boat

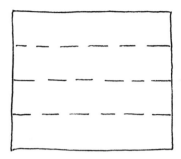

Fold a square piece of paper in half and then fold in half again. Unfold.

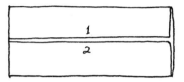

Fold as shown and crease.

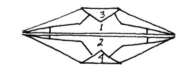

Fold end flaps toward the center.

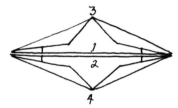

Then fold again as shown.

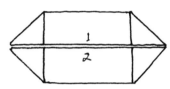

Fold points 3 and 4 as shown.

Fold paper back in half on center fold.

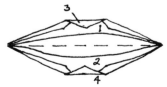

Take hold of 1 and 2 and pull outward slightly, holding points 3 and 4, and turn inside out.

Smooth out with your fingers.

76. Draw a Bible

To make your Bible, fill in each small square in the box at the bottom of the page with the same shapes as the small squares in the box at the top.

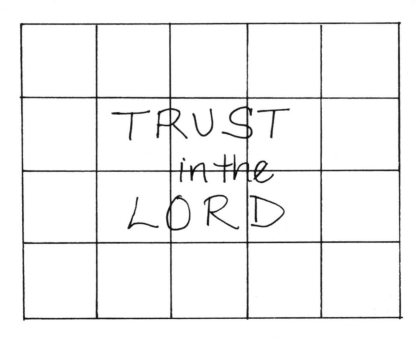

77. Change a Letter

Change **far** to   ___ ___ ___ ___

Change **well** to   ___ ___ ___ ___

Change **table** to   ___ ___ ___ ___ ___

Change **moss** to   ___ ___ ___ ___

Change **dove** to   ___ ___ ___ ___

Change **look** to   ___ ___ ___ ___

Change **seven** to   ___ ___ ___ ___ ___

78. Church Window Maze

Find your way through the church window.

79. Picture to Color

80. Love Maze

The Bible says we should love each other. Find your way through the maze by spelling the word **LOVE** over and over again.

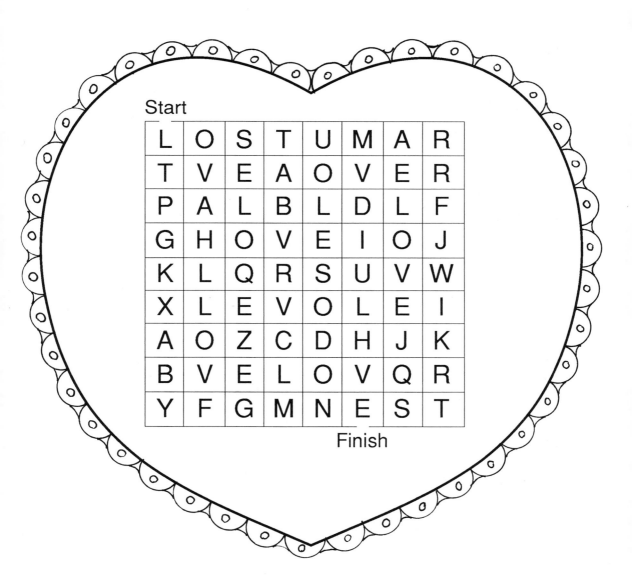

Start

L	O	S	T	U	M	A	R
T	V	E	A	O	V	E	R
P	A	L	B	L	D	L	F
G	H	O	V	E	I	O	J
K	L	Q	R	S	U	V	W
X	L	E	V	O	L	E	I
A	O	Z	C	D	H	J	K
B	V	E	L	O	V	Q	R
Y	F	G	M	N	E	S	T

Finish

ANSWERS

9. THE ANGEL'S MESSAGE

10. LUKE 19:10

FOR THE SON OF MAN CAME TO SEEK
AND TO SAVE WHAT WAS LOST. LUKE
19:10

16. THE GIFT OF GOD'S LOVE

JESUS

20. ANGELS' MESSAGE

GLORY TO GOD IN THE HIGHEST.

23. JESUS' AGE WHEN HE DIED

$3 + 7 + 2 + 4 + 5 + 1 + 3 + 8 = 33$

25. FOR WHOM DID JESUS DIE?

PILOT	GRANDMA	CLERK
DOCTOR	YOU	PLUMBER
AUNT	MOTHER	FARMER
POLICEMEN	GRANDPA	BEGGERS
PASTOR	ARTIST	NURSE
UNCLE	MISSIONARY	STUDENT
TEACHER	BROTHER	
SISTER	FRIENDS	
DAD	NEIGHBORS	

30. MARK 6:1–8

31. ANGEL AT THE TOMB

HE IS NOT HERE; HE HAS RISEN, JUST AS
HE SAID.

33. JESUS SAID . . .

GO INTO ALL THE WORLD AND PREACH
THE GOOD NEWS TO ALL CREATION.

34. WHAT HAPPENED AT PENTECOST?

ALL OF THEM WERE FILLED WITH THE
HOLY SPIRIT AND BEGAN TO SPEAK IN
OTHER TONGUES AS THE SPIRIT EN-
ABLED THEM.

35. JESUS' PROMISE

COME AGAIN

37. CHRIST'S RETURN

38. A PROMISE
HE WILL COME AGAIN

41. COUNT THE HEARTS
67 hearts

42. HEART WREATH
A FRIEND LOVES AT ALL TIMES.

44. A GOOD RULE
GIVE THANKS IN ALL CIRCUMSTANCES.

45. PSALM 107:1
GIVE THANKS TO THE LORD FOR HE IS GOOD.

46. DINNER WORD SCRAMBLE
TURKEY
CORN
POTATOES
BREAD
PIE
DRESSING
MILK
SALAD
BUTTER
PEAS

47. THANKSGIVING WORD SCRAMBLE
SCHOOL
HOME
FOOD
CLOTHES
CHURCH
FRIENDS
BIBLE
JESUS
PARENTS

52. SALVATION MESSAGE
BELIEVE ON THE LORD JESUS

53. LUKE 10:2
HARVEST, PLENTIFUL, WORKERS, ASK, LORD, HARVEST, WORKERS, HARVEST

54. CODED MESSAGE
WE BELIEVE IT IS THROUGH THE GRACE OF OUR LORD JESUS THAT WE ARE SAVED.

58. THE BEST GIFT
CROSS, ANGEL, SALT, VALENTINE, BAT, TREE, PIG, DONUT, PENCIL

63. LUKE 21:33
HEAVEN AND EARTH WILL PASS AWAY, BUT MY WORDS WILL NEVER PASS AWAY.

65. WHO FORGIVES SIN?
JESUS

68. MISSING LETTERS
CHRIST DIED FOR OUR SINS ACCORDING TO THE SCRIPTURES.

71. HIDDEN LETTERS
HOLY SPIRIT

72. LUKE 2:10
BUT THE ANGEL SAID TO THEM, "DO NOT BE AFRAID. I BRING YOU GOOD NEWS OF GREAT JOY."

73. FREEDOM TO WORSHIP
AMERICA

77. CHANGE A LETTER
STAR, BELL, STABLE, CROSS, LOVE, BOOK, HEAVEN